D0791961

DISCARD

SCHOOL
LIBRARY

HOLLY CEFREY

Epidemics
Deadly Diseases
Throughout History

AIDS

SAN LEANDRO
LIBRARY
HIGH SCHOOL

The Rosen Publishing Group, Inc.
New York

To R.C., Ethan, Elaine, and Dean

Published in 2001 by The Rosen Publishing Group, Inc.
29 East 21st Street, New York, NY 10010

Copyright © 2001 by The Rosen Publishing Group, Inc.

First Edition

All rights reserved. No part of this book may be reproduced in any form without permission in writing from the publisher, except by a reviewer.

Library of Congress Cataloging-in-Publication Data

Cefrey, Holly.
    AIDS / by Holly Cefrey. — 1st ed.
        p. cm. — (Epidemics)
        ISBN 0-8239-3344-X
        1. AIDS (Disease)—Juvenile literature. [1. AIDS (Disease) 2. Diseases.] I. Title. II. Epidemics.
RC607.A26 C44 2000
616.97'92—dc21

                                                    00-010785

Cover image: An electron micrograph of the surface of a T-lymphocyte white blood cell (green) with AIDS viruses (pink) budding from it. An infected T-cell typically has a lumpy appearance (as shown here).

Manufactured in the United States of America

CONTENTS

Introduction   5

Chapter 1 How HIV Causes AIDS   10

Chapter 2 The History of AIDS
                    and HIV   23

Chapter 3 The Worldwide AIDS
                    Epidemic   37

Chapter 4 Diagnosis of AIDS   40

Chapter 5 Treatment, Research,
                    and Prevention   50

                 Glossary   57

                 For More Information   59

                 For Further Reading   61

                 Index   62

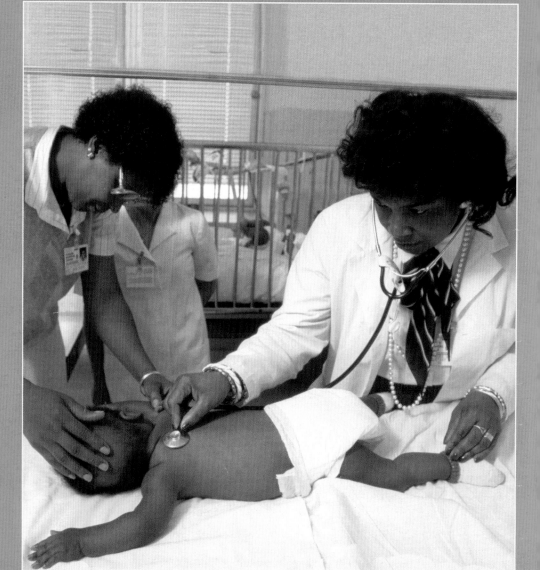

Babies born to HIV-positive mothers are often born HIV-positive as well. Mothers can also pass HIV on to their babies through breast-feeding.

INTRODUCTION

"I grew up in a small town where everybody knew everybody else. My father was an artist, and I had a very creative and liberal upbringing. Dad encouraged me to talk about anything. Even though he grew up in our town, he was seen as 'different,' because he was a divorced single parent. Most of the locals were very conservative.

"I was seven years old when I first heard about AIDS. All the locals were talking about a rare 'gay' cancer. I knew that cancer made people sick, but I wasn't really sure what 'gay' meant. Over the next year, I heard other words, such as homosexual, contagious, and plague. Every time I heard a word that I didn't understand, I would ask Dad, or his best friend, Tom, to explain. When I asked him questions about AIDS, Dad said, 'I'll have to start researching AIDS because I want you to be fully informed.'

"I noticed that Dad's information about AIDS was different from what everybody in town was saying about it. They claimed that God had put a curse on homosexuals and that people were becoming sick because their lifestyle was a sin. But Dad said that people other than homosexuals developed AIDS. He also taught me that AIDS was a disease, not a curse.

"After my father started writing for our local newspaper about AIDS issues and awareness, the locals started treating us badly. One neighbor accused my dad and Tom of being a gay couple. Kids at school said that I could make other people sick because my dad had AIDS. My family was treated as if we were contagious.

"My town had turned into a horrible place full of paranoia. My dad wasn't mad that people thought he was gay, but he was mad that they let their fear and ignorance keep them from knowing the truth about AIDS. We moved away, but I often wonder if those people ever learned that the things they were saying were hurtful and wrong.

"My experience with AIDS and that little town taught me a lot about life. I learned about

sexuality, religion, discrimination, hate, and ignorance. I also learned that it's hurtful to condemn someone for his or her lifestyle or beliefs. Finding out the facts about something before forming an opinion is the smartest thing to do."
—Chris, AIDS activist

AIDS Facts

AIDS, or acquired immunodeficiency syndrome, is a disease. "Acquired" means that the disease is not naturally found in the body. "Immunodeficiency" is a combination of the words "immune" and "deficiency." It means that the body's immune system is not working well—it has a deficiency. "Syndrome" means that there is a group of symptoms, or signs of an illness, that go along with having the disease. When a person has AIDS, his or her immune system becomes weak. When the immune system is weakened, a person can develop any number of serious illnesses.

AIDS is caused by a virus. Viruses are commonly found in humans and cause illnesses such as colds or flu. Viruses cannot survive by themselves. They must live inside the cells of another living organism, or a host, in order to survive. Once a virus has a host cell, it begins to multiply so rapidly that the cell becomes full of the virus. Eventually the cell bursts like a balloon,

releasing the virus into surrounding body areas where it finds other cells to live in.

The virus that causes AIDS is the human immuno-deficiency virus, or HIV. A person infected with HIV is said to be HIV-positive. A person can be infected with HIV and infect others even if there are no symptoms of illness. HIV can live in a person's body for years without causing any symptoms. AIDS develops at the advanced stages of HIV infection.

HIV on the Attack

Human beings are constantly exposed to viruses and foreign invaders, which are any organisms not naturally found within the body. The immune system acts as a defense against all of the invaders that attack the body. HIV attacks and weakens a person's immune system.

The immune system can be compared to an army, made up of cells that protect the body. There are several different kinds of cells in the immune army, each with their own job to do. Helper T cells, B cells, and T4 cells scan the body for invaders. When they encounter an invader, they send out chemical signals that alert and activate the rest of the immune army. B cells make antibodies, the proteins that destroy invaders. Killer T cells, or T8 cells, attach themselves to cells that are infected with an invader. They release chemicals to destroy the infected or abnormal cell.

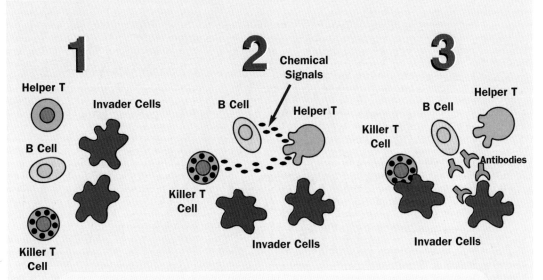

Helper T cells, B cells, and Killer T cells scan the body for invaders. When one is found, the Helper T cells release chemical signals that alert and activate the other cells in an immune response.

HIV can attack the immune system cells for months or years without a person knowing it. The strength of a person's immune system depends on a number of factors, including age, traits that he or she inherited from a parent, general health, and illnesses that he or she has been exposed to before. The differences in each person regarding each of these factors is why some people get sick quickly while others are affected only mildly by the same infection. No matter how strong a person's immune system is to begin with, eventually HIV will weaken it so much that the body can no longer defend itself from disease.

1

HOW HIV CAUSES AIDS

In order for an HIV-infected person to develop AIDS, certain infections must also be present in addition to the HIV infection. These infections are called opportunistic infections. Opportunistic infections are illnesses that rarely cause disease or harm in persons with healthy immune systems. In people with advanced HIV, however, opportunistic infections can develop into severe or fatal infections. They are called opportunistic infections because they use the opportunity of a weakened immune system to attack.

There are twenty-six opportunistic infections that doctors recognize as an indication that a person's HIV infection has advanced into AIDS. Certain kinds of cancer are included on the list of opportunistic infections. People with AIDS often have opportunistic infections that develop in the eyes, lungs, brain, and other organs. These illnesses cause symptoms such as coughing, shortness of breath, short-term memory loss, loss of vision, weight loss, lack of energy, nausea, vomiting, stomach cramps, or seizures.

A physician can also make an AIDS diagnosis based on the results of blood tests. The physician examines the T cell count, or the number of T cells present in the blood of a patient with HIV. In a person with a healthy immune system, the T cell count usually ranges from 500 to 1,500 cells. If a patient has HIV and a T cell count that is less than 200 cells, a physician will make the diagnosis of AIDS, even if the patient seems perfectly healthy.

Telltale Symptoms

Even though an infected person can live for years without developing symptoms of HIV, there are some common warning signs of HIV infection that may occur. Even if you suffer from one or more of the common warning signs, it does not mean that you have HIV. Many other illnesses have the same symptoms. Only a doctor can diagnose an illness.

One of the first warnings that HIV-infected people experience is swollen lymph nodes. Lymph nodes

1980
Thirty-one mysterious deaths with similar symptoms are reported in the United States.

1981
A new illness is named GRID, or gay-related immune deficiency.

1982-1983
GRID infects people other than homosexuals. The Centers for Disease Control use the term "AIDS" to describe the new illness. Luc Montagnier discovers a virus that is linked to AIDS.

are small, bean-shaped organs that are part of the immune system. The lymph nodes that you can feel are in the neck, armpits, and groin area. There are also nodes deep inside the body. Lymph nodes store the army of immune cells, which trap and destroy invaders. A lymph node swells as the army of immune cells attacks the invaders that are trapped inside of it.

Possible warning signs of HIV infection include frequent fevers, rapid weight loss, unexplained fatigue, breathing difficulties, excessive sweating, diarrhea that lasts longer than a week, white spots or sores in the mouth and throat, pneumonia, memory loss, vision problems, and red, pink, purple, or brown blotches on or under the skin.

1986
The virus that causes AIDS is given the name human immunodeficiency virus, or HIV.

1996
Researchers discover a herpes virus that causes Kaposi's sarcoma.

1999
Researchers link HIV to SIV, or simian immunodeficiency virus.

How HIV Spreads

Scientists have researched how HIV is transmitted, or spread. Studies show that HIV can infect anyone and be spread to anyone. We also know that HIV is passed from an infected person to an uninfected person through certain body fluids. Body fluids that can spread HIV include blood, semen and preseminal fluid (fluid that is released prior to semen), vaginal secretions and menstrual blood, and breast milk.

A person can come into contact with the body fluids of an HIV-infected person in a variety of ways. Researchers have isolated the kinds of ways or activities in which HIV is transmitted through infected body fluids. Activities that allow the

Using condoms can help prevent the spread of HIV during sexual intercourse.

exchange of infected bodily fluids include unprotected sexual contact, sharing hypodermic needles, sharing needles used for tattoos or piercings, pregnancy, giving birth, and breast-feeding.

Unprotected Sexual Contact

HIV can be spread sexually to and from people of either gender: from male to female, male to male, female to male, and, most rarely, female to female. When an infected partner has sexual intercourse with an uninfected partner, HIV can be passed through any of the body fluids involved in sexual contact: semen, pre-seminal fluid, and vaginal secretions.

Unprotected sexual contact means that a condom (male birth control device) is not used. Sexual contact includes anything relating to the anus, vagina, penis, or mouth (oral sexual contact). The more sexual partners that a person has, the higher his or her chances of encountering someone who is infected with HIV. People who are infected with HIV might have unprotected sex, not knowing that they have the disease.

Sharing needles with an HIV-infected person is extremely risky behavior.

Sharing Hypodermic Needles

Sharing needles with an HIV-infected person, even once, is enough of an opportunity for HIV to travel from one person to the next. Needles used for injecting substances such as heroin or steroids can spread HIV when shared by more than one user. Sharing a needle is dangerous because blood from

an HIV-infected person can stay in the needle, which is then injected into the next person.

Tattoos and Piercings

Tattoos and piercings require the use of needles. Needles can be contaminated with HIV if they were used on an infected person. HIV can be removed from tattoo and piercing needles if they are sterilized, or cleansed thoroughly so that all germs are removed. Professional tattoo and piercing studios have special machines that when used properly will sterilize the equipment.

Even the low level of HIV found in breast milk is enough to infect a baby.

Pregnancy, Birth, and Breast-Feeding

A woman with HIV can pass HIV along to her baby during pregnancy. A mother can also pass HIV on to her baby through breast-feeding. Breast milk doesn't contain as much HIV as blood, semen, or vaginal secretions, but even a small amount of HIV in the milk is enough to infect a baby.

How HIV Is Not Spread

Research on HIV has shown that certain body fluids do not pass HIV along to another person, even though the fluids come from an infected person. Substances or chemicals in these body fluids do not allow the HIV to be infectious. Body fluids that do not transmit HIV from an infected person include tears, saliva, sweat, urine, and feces.

Research has also shown that certain activities do not transmit HIV from one person to another. Activities that are safe, even when they are done by or with an HIV-infected person, include shaking or holding hands, hugging, coughing, sneezing, closed mouth or "social" kissing, swimming in pools, using public toilets, and sharing household objects such as eating utensils.

Fact or Myth

When a disease occurs, there are issues about the disease that are proven by science to be true, but there are also issues that take time to study and

prove. While waiting for absolute answers to unproven issues, people can get confused. The most up-to-date research provides some clarity when dealing with the following issues about the spread of HIV and AIDS.

Giving Blood to, or Receiving Blood from, a Hospital or Blood Bank

Giving blood is an important and safe activity. When you give blood, your blood will be given to people who have been injured or to people undergoing surgery. You cannot get AIDS by giving blood to a blood bank or hospital.

In the years before 1985, there were some cases of people who developed HIV after receiving someone's donated blood. This was a time when donated blood wasn't yet suspected as a source of HIV. The infected people who gave the blood might not have known that they had HIV, and neither did the hospitals. Today, blood donors are carefully screened. The donated blood is treated to ensure that the blood does not contain any viruses, including HIV. Today, transmission of HIV through donated blood is extremely rare.

Insect Bites

HIV is not transmitted or spread by insect bites. Insects that bite humans, such as mosquitoes or

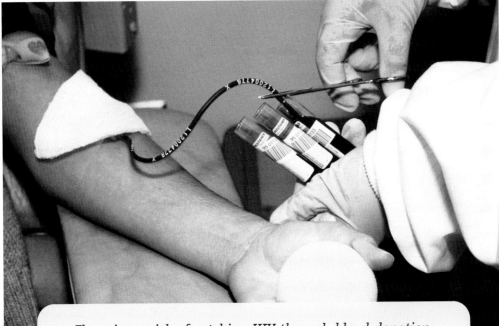

There is no risk of catching HIV through blood donation.

bedbugs, do not transmit HIV. HIV cannot reproduce or survive inside of these insects. Even if an insect draws blood from an HIV-infected person, the bug will not get infected or pass the infected blood on to another human.

Prolonged Kissing

Researchers have located HIV in the saliva of infected people, but there is no evidence to show that the virus is actually spread through saliva. Saliva contains substances that stop HIV from being infectious (able to infect). Closed-mouth kissing with an infected person is still considered safe. Caution should be taken if

HIV cannot be passed from one person to another through "social" kissing or hand-holding.

either partner has sores or wounds in or around the mouth where infectious body fluids could enter in the case of open mouth, or French, kissing.

Visits to the Doctor or Dentist

The chances of getting AIDS by visiting your doctor's or dentist's office are extremely small. When your doctor or dentist treats a patient with AIDS, special precautions are taken before, during, and after the infected patient's treatment. Most health care providers follow strict infection-control procedures that protect both patients and health care providers by preventing any transmission of HIV.

Some medical professionals believe that HIV is related to SIV, or simian immunodeficiency virus, a virus that naturally occurs among apes and that may have its origins in Africa.

2

THE HISTORY OF AIDS AND HIV

HIV is an acquired virus, which means that a person has to do certain things in order to be infected by it. How and when the first human became infected with HIV are questions that scientists have been researching for close to twenty years. After studying HIV, some members of the medical profession believe that HIV is a descendant or a relative of SIV (simian immunodeficiency virus). SIV is a virus that naturally occurs among apes and monkeys. If this belief is correct, it means that the first humans infected with HIV were infected through contact with infected simians.

Research has shown that HIV is a virus that can mutate, or change itself in order to survive. There are a couple of different mutations,

or types, of HIV, and they are distinguished by the way in which they infect a person. In general, when speaking of any HIV type, the term "HIV" can be used. Researchers are also trying to prove guesses, or theories, about how simians could have infected humans with HIV.

Infection Through a Pet or Food Source

Some researchers think that the first HIV infection in a human happened during a time when chimpanzees and sooty mangabeys were kept as pets or butchered for food. It is believed that this might have occurred sometime between 1940 and 1950. HIV could have been passed to a human through certain types of contact with an infected simian.

Infection Through a Vaccine

Another theory is that humans became infected with HIV through polio vaccines. A vaccine is medicine that is designed to increase a person's immunity to a certain illness. Polio vaccines were given to large numbers of people during the 1950s and 1960s. The kidneys of lab monkeys were used in the preparation of the polio vaccines. The theory is that the vaccines were contaminated with HIV because the monkey kidneys that were used in the preparation were already infected with SIV.

HIV and AIDS in Human History

Before the 1980s, AIDS did not have a name or a known cause, but it was occurring nonetheless. It wasn't until 1982 that this mysterious disease was given a name. The term "AIDS" was first used in 1982 by the Centers for Disease Control (CDC) to describe a new disease affecting people's immune systems.

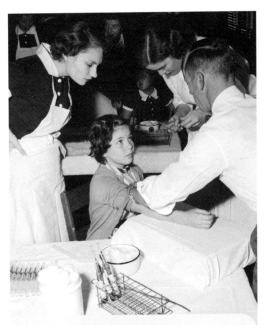

HIV in humans may be the result of the polio vaccine.

Through modern tests, scientists have been able to trace cases of AIDS that occurred prior to 1982. There are three confirmed cases of death due to HIV infection that occurred prior to the 1980s, before anyone knew about HIV and AIDS.

1959

An old plasma sample, taken in 1959 from a man who died in central Africa, was tested for the presence of HIV. Dr. David Ho and Dr. Tuofu Zhu of the Aaron Diamond AIDS Research Center and Andre Nahmias of Emory University succeeded in finding the presence of the virus in the plasma sample. Researchers believe that this type of HIV may date back to the 1940s.

1969

Tissue samples, taken in 1969 from an African-American teenager who died in St. Louis, were tested for the presence of HIV. The samples were tested because the teenager had died from AIDS-like symptoms. The HIV virus or a very close relative of the virus was found in the tissues. The findings indicate that a type of HIV was present in the United States before the 1970s.

1976

Tissue samples were taken in 1976 from a Norwegian family of three who died of AIDS-like symptoms, and tested for the presence of HIV. The father of the family was a sailor who sailed to Africa and became infected with different kinds of diseases at least twice. The tissues from the father, mother, and daughter all contained a type of HIV that is common to West Africa.

The Early 1980s—
Trying to Understand AIDS

The spread of AIDS was an epidemic, or a wave of disease, that affected and still affects many people. The history of the AIDS epidemic begins in the early 1980s and is full of mystery, scandal, and scientific successes.

In 1980, there were thirty-one mysterious deaths in the United States. The deceased had all suffered from similar symptoms. By 1981, the CDC reported an unusual occurrence of a rare cancer, called Kaposi's sarcoma, in otherwise healthy gay men. Kaposi's sarcoma had developed in forty-one gay men from New York and California. At the same time, a rare pneumonia, or lung infection, was occurring in the gay community. Physicians believed that a new immune deficiency was developing among the gay community and called it GRID, or gay-related immune deficiency. By the end of 1981, there were 422 cases of diagnosed GRID, and 159 people had already died from it.

In 1982, GRID was also infecting hemophiliacs, or people whose blood does not clot. Hemophiliacs receive donated blood in the event that they are injured. The CDC linked the disease to blood and found that there might be a problem with the blood supply.

When a new disease strikes on an epidemic scale, there is a race in the global scientific community to find out what is causing the disease. The race for the discovery of the cause of AIDS created conflict between two countries and two of their best researchers.

In May of 1983, a virologist, or a person who studies viruses, named Luc Montagnier claimed that he had found a virus that was linked to AIDS.

He and his team from the Pasteur Institute in France had found a virus in the swollen lymph nodes of a patient. Montagnier named the virus LAV, which is short for lymphadenopathy associated virus. Lymphadenopathy is one of the first symptoms found in HIV patients who are progressing toward the development of AIDS.

Luc Montagnier

In April of 1984, the United States government held a press conference at which the secretary of health claimed that Robert Gallo, of the National Cancer Institute, had isolated a virus that caused AIDS, and its name was HTLV-III. The announcement of the discovered virus was also followed by the announcement that Gallo had invented a blood test that would detect HIV antibodies. At the time of this press conference, there was little knowledge that the discovery of the virus had taken place nearly a year before in France.

Commercial kits for the antibody HIV test were licensed. The Pasteur Institute filed a lawsuit against the National Cancer Institute, claiming that they deserved a share of the profits from the tests. This lawsuit was filed because when Montagnier discovered the virus, he sent samples to Gallo's lab. It is reported that the two researchers had plans to publish and announce their findings together. Two weeks before the 1984 press conference, the media found out that a cause for AIDS had been found. Before Robert Gallo knew it, he was sitting at a press conference, without the presence of Montagnier or the Pasteur Institute to share in the credit of discovery.

Robert Gallo

In 1992, Montagnier and Gallo agreed that the viruses they had found were one and the same. That same year, the United States acknowledged that the Pasteur Institute was responsible for the isolation of the virus that causes AIDS—not Robert Gallo. A settlement between the two researchers was reached where they could call themselves codiscoverers.

The GRID-infected hemophiliacs had received contaminated blood, which caused their illness. Because the illness was not exclusive to the gay community, the name was changed from GRID to AIDS.

In 1983, after two women developed the disease after being infected by their male partners, it became known that heterosexuals who had not received donated blood could develop AIDS. Because the direct cause of AIDS was not yet known, the fear of becoming infected was a major issue for many people. AIDS had already been reported in thirty-two other countries.

In the early part of 1983, a doctor named Luc Montagnier of the Pasteur Institute in France declared that he had discovered a virus that was associated with AIDS. This virus later became known as HIV. By the end of 1983, there were 1,614 new cases of AIDS infection and 619 people had died from the disease.

The Epidemic Grows

In 1984, a man named Gaetan Dugas died from AIDS. It is believed that he played a major role in the spread of AIDS in the gay community. Gaetan was a flight attendant who was based in New York. When Gaetan was interviewed in 1982, he disclosed the fact that he had an average of 250 encounters of unprotected sex per year. Between the years of 1978 and 1982, Gaetan estimated that he had unprotected sex with 750 different men. A large number of AIDS patients over the following years were linked to Gaetan. They either had unprotected sex with Gaetan or had sex with someone who had been a sexual partner to Gaetan. Gaetan Dugas is also referred to as "patient zero" by some researchers. Some people believe that this is an unfair title because it suggests that Gaetan is the origin of the spread of AIDS in America.

The year 1985 brought the AIDS epidemic to a deeper level of awareness. The legendary film star Rock Hudson announced that he had AIDS, and later that same year he died from related illnesses. The death of such a major public figure made AIDS a household topic. Also, a teenager named Ryan White, who had contracted AIDS through a blood transfusion, was barred from attending public school. The fact that a youth could have AIDS and be barred from receiving an education sparked several debates over the rights of the infected and the uninfected. It was also during this year that condoms were proven to be effective in preventing the sexual transmission of HIV.

The first time that the term "HIV" was used to describe the virus that causes AIDS was in 1986. It was determined that Gallo's HTLV-III and Montagnier's LAV were the same virus. An international committee ruled that both names should be replaced with HIV.

Ryan White, who contracted HIV through a blood transfusion, fought to stay in school. He died in 1990.

The Late 1980s—
The Government Acts

During the late eighties, the United States government started to put effort into public awareness and education about AIDS. Although press coverage of HIV and AIDS was becoming more common, United States president Ronald Reagan had yet to mention the word "AIDS" in public. In 1987, President Reagan made his first speech about the AIDS epidemic. The following are some other notable moments of the late 1980s.

⊙ The U.S. surgeon general published a report on AIDS, which called for sex education (1986).

- The first anti-HIV drug, called AZT, was approved by the Food and Drug Administration (FDA) (1987).

- *And the Band Played On,* Randy Shilts' account of the early days of the AIDS epidemic, was published (1987).

- The United States barred travelers with HIV from entering the country (1987).

- The AIDS Memorial Quilt was started in San Francisco (1987).

- The U.S. government mailed 107 million copies of the surgeon general's booklet "Understanding AIDS" to the public (1988).

The AIDS Memorial Quilt was started in San Francisco in 1987.

- The price of AZT treatment, around $12,000 a year, was lowered by 20 percent after many protests by AIDS activists (1989).

- The FDA approved four drugs that treat opportunistic infections (1989).

The 1990s—A Time of Progress

The 1990s brought about increased public awareness of AIDS. People were educated about the fact that AIDS was everybody's disease, and that HIV could infect anyone. In 1991, athlete Magic Johnson announced that he was HIV-positive. This event caused people to take HIV antibody tests in record numbers. Issues relating to AIDS health care reform, funding, and social acceptance became important to the general public. Important moments of progress for AIDS awareness in the 1990s include:

- Ronald Reagan apologized for neglecting the AIDS epidemic while he was president (1990).

- Congress passed the Ryan White CARE Act, named after the AIDS activist who was infected and denied access to a public education (1990).

- Congress passed the Americans with Disabilities Act. This act prohibits discrimination against anyone with HIV or AIDS (1990).

- The red ribbon was chosen as a symbol for AIDS awareness (1991).

- The largest AIDS benefit in the world was held in memory of Freddie Mercury, lead singer of the band Queen (1992).

Since the AIDS epidemic began, more than 16 million people have lost their lives to AIDS and related illnesses. The following list of well-known people who have died from AIDS and AIDS-related illnesses is a reminder of the fact that AIDS can affect anyone from any background or circumstance.

1985 Rock Hudson, legendary film star
1987 Michael Bennett, Broadway director of *A Chorus Line*
1989 Robert Mapplethorpe, controversial artist
1990 Ryan White, teenage AIDS activist who fought to attend public school
1991 Freddie Mercury, lead singer of the band Queen
1992 Robert Reed, actor who played Mike Brady on *The Brady Bunch*
1993 Rudolf Nureyev, world-renowned ballet dancer
1994 Eric "Eazy-E" Wright, rap artist
1996 Peter Adair, independent filmmaker
2000 Ofra Haza, popular singer and musician

Artist Eric "Eazy-E" Wright, a founding member of rap group NWA, died of AIDS in 1994.

- Four French blood bank workers were sent to prison for allowing HIV-tainted blood into blood banks (1993).

- President Clinton held the first White House AIDS Summit (1995).

The 1990s were also a time of scientific successes in the battle against HIV and AIDS.

- The first reports of combination drug treatments that are successful against AIDS were published (1992).

- The CDC changed the definition of AIDS to include opportunistic infections (1993).

- Researchers discovered a herpes virus that causes Kaposi's sarcoma (1996).

- The CDC reported that annual AIDS and AIDS-related deaths in the United States dropped 19 percent (1997).

- The CDC reported that annual AIDS and AIDS-related deaths dropped 47 percent (1998).

- Researchers linked HIV to SIV, or simian immuno-deficiency virus (1999).

3

THE WORLDWIDE AIDS EPIDEMIC

By the year 2005, there will be more than 100 million people infected with HIV worldwide. When a disease infects and threatens the lives of such a large number of people, it is considered to be an epidemic. In some areas of the world, AIDS-related deaths are reported in alarmingly high numbers. Africa, India, and East Asia are areas that have been hit especially hard by the epidemic.

Africa

Almost 24 million Africans have HIV or AIDS. Another 11,000 Africans are infected with HIV each day. One million of the nearly 24 million infected Africans are children. The AIDS epidemic has left 11 million African children orphaned. African deaths due to AIDS will soon surpass 20 million. These deaths make up more than 80 percent of world-wide AIDS deaths. Each day, AIDS kills nearly 5,000 Africans.

India

It is estimated that 3.7 million people in India are HIV-infected. It is also believed that thousands of cases of AIDS in India remain undiagnosed. In some areas of the country, one out of every fifty pregnant women is HIV-positive. By the end of 2000, the cost of damages due to AIDS will be over $11 billion in India.

Thousands of cases of AIDS in India may remain undiagnosed.

East Asia

At the end of 1999, nearly 6.5 million East Asian people were living with HIV infection. It has also been estimated that by 2005, the number of AIDS deaths in East Asia will equal those in Africa. Transmission by heterosexual sex is the most common way that AIDS is transmitted in East Asia.

Orphans of the AIDS Epidemic

At least 6.5 million East Asian people are HIV infected.

In countries where large numbers of adults have died because of AIDS-related illnesses, many important roles in society, such as educators, health care workers, and law enforcement officers, are left unfilled. Without enough people in these important roles, the quality of life in these countries declines rapidly.

A large number of adult deaths means that many children will be left orphaned. Children who have no relatives who are able to care for them may be left to fend for themselves. Orphaned children are also at a greater risk of becoming infected with HIV. Without parents or guardians, the children may be more likely to be exposed to dangers like sexual abuse, which may lead to HIV infection.

4

DIAGNOSIS OF AIDS

In order for a doctor to diagnose a patient with HIV or AIDS, the patient must take medical blood tests. Anyone can be infected with HIV. Since HIV-infected people often lack symptoms for several years, a person must examine his or her past and present activities when considering the possibility of having HIV or AIDS. A person should take an HIV blood test if he or she:

- Had unprotected sex with an infected partner
- Had unprotected sex with someone whom he or she didn't know very well
- Had more than one sexual partner
- Used needles or shared them with others

40

☹ Received tattoos or piercings from a used, unclean needle

☺ Received blood donations between 1977 and 1985

If a person is doing or has done any of these things, it's a good idea for him or her to speak with a doctor about taking an HIV test. More than 100,000 adults in the United States may be living with HIV without knowing it. These people may be taking risks that will spread HIV to other unsuspecting people.

When to Take an HIV Test

A good time to take an HIV test is anywhere from three to six months after realizing that you have put yourself at risk for infection. The most common tests used are called HIV antibody blood tests, which test the levels of antibodies in the blood. Antibodies are proteins that the body produces in order to fight infection. It can take anywhere from three to six months after initially being infected with HIV for the antibodies to develop to a detectable level. The average time for the antibodies to develop is around twenty-five days, and in extremely rare cases it can take longer than six months.

Types of HIV Tests

In addition to the HIV antibody blood tests, there are other tests that a person can take to test for infection. Most tests are conducted in a hospital, doctor's office, HIV testing center, or health clinic. There are also tests that you can take at home. Testing will most likely be accompanied by counseling, which will answer any questions that you may have.

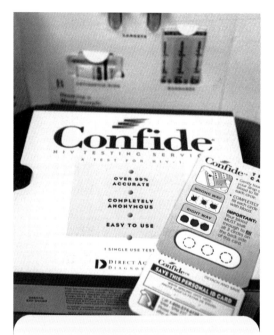

There are several HIV home-testing kits available to the public.

At certain testing centers, you can take any of the HIV tests in two different ways: anonymously or confidentially. Anonymously means that your name is not attached to any samples that will be taken from you, and only you will know the results of your tests. Confidentially means that your name and results are taken for a record. The only people who have access to your name and results are the medical staff and possibly your state's health department. If you sign any release forms, your test results can be released to your regular doctor. If your doctor writes the results in your medical record, third parties, such as insurance companies, health care workers, and employers, can obtain access to this information.

HIV Antibody Blood Tests

Antibody blood tests are used to detect HIV antibodies in the bloodstream. Three common antibody tests are the EIA, the ELISA, and the Western Blot. The results are close to 100 percent accurate. Finding out the results from an antibody test usually takes one to two weeks. Another antibody blood test that produces quicker results is called the rapid test. Results from the rapid test can be obtained in as little as five minutes.

Testing for HIV at Home

HIV home test kits can be purchased by mail, on the Internet, and at health clinics. To take the test, you prick your finger and then place drops of your blood onto a sponge. The sponge is placed in a plastic container that contains a special paper. You add a developing solution to the container to determine if you have HIV. Although home test kits of this kind seem easy and fast, they are not as accurate as the tests

that are sent to a laboratory. The FDA has not approved any home test kits.

There are other tests called home blood collection systems. These tests are different from home test kits because your blood is sent to a lab for analysis. For this kind of test, you prick your finger and place blood droplets on a special card. You mail the special card to a laboratory where it is tested. The only FDA-approved home blood collection system is called the Home Access Express HIV-1 test, which can be found at most drug stores. The results usually take one to three weeks.

HIV Test Results

Taking an HIV test can be a difficult and nerve-wracking experience. Anyone who undergoes testing for HIV should seek counseling before, during, and after, if possible. Speaking with a counselor can help you to understand results, prevention methods, treatment methods, and general information about HIV or AIDS.

If You Have HIV

When test results come back positive, it means that there are HIV antibodies present in the blood. The patient will have to take another test to ensure that the first test was correct. If the second test comes back positive, it means that the patient will be diagnosed with HIV. A person who receives a positive diagnosis is called HIV-positive. Being HIV-positive means that you can pass HIV along to other people.

If a person is diagnosed with HIV, it is important that he or she take steps toward a healthier, safer lifestyle. Early medical treatment may delay the development of AIDS, and possibly prevent other severe illnesses from developing.

If You Don't Have HIV

When results from a test come back negative, it means that HIV antibodies were not detected in the blood. A negative result does not mean that you cannot get HIV or become infected with it in the future. A negative test result may also mean that you haven't developed the antibodies yet, so it is wise to take the HIV test again about six months later to ensure that the test didn't miss HIV antibodies.

False Positive and False Negative

There is always a chance that the results from HIV tests will be wrong. A false positive result occurs when the test shows the presence of infection due to a virus or infection other than HIV. More common is

Regardless of the possible outcome, anyone who is tested for HIV should try to seek counseling before, during, and after the test.

a false negative result. A negative result can be wrong if the test was taken before HIV antibodies had time to develop in an infected person. In this case, the negative result is false because HIV is present, but at the time of the test, the HIV antibodies could not be detected.

Stages of HIV and AIDS

When a person has tested positive for HIV but does not suffer any of the symptoms, the disease is in its asymptomatic stage. "Asymptomatic" means without symptoms. Even though there are no symptoms, the virus is reproducing around 10 billion HIV germs a day.

The next stage of HIV infection is called the early symptomatic stage. This means that HIV is in the early stages of showing some symptoms. A person in this stage might experience fever, night sweats, weight loss, fatigue, difficulty breathing, swollen lymph nodes, diarrhea, pneumonia, or vision problems.

In the late symptomatic stage, the immune system of an infected person begins to weaken. An infected person might experience the symptoms of the early symptomatic stage more frequently, as well as new symptoms such as shingles (a disease of the skin), cancerous growths, and AIDS wasting syndrome (extreme weight loss).

AIDS-Related Cancers

Kaposi's sarcoma (KS) is a cancer that usually appears on the skin but can also appear on the linings of the digestive track and the lungs. It causes purplish markings, called lesions, to appear on the body. KS was a rare form of cancer before the 1980s. Now, most cases of KS occur in people with AIDS.

Lymphoma is cancer of the lymphocytes, or white blood cells. The white blood cells are the most important cells of the immune system. Lymphoma can develop in a few lymph nodes or at several places in the body at once. People with advanced HIV have a higher than average risk of developing lymphoma.

Women with HIV are at increased risk to develop cervical cancer. There are no symptoms associated with the early stages of cervical cancer, so women must take yearly tests in order to know if they have developed the disease.

Mental Disorders

Persons with AIDS are at an increased risk of suffering from certain mental disorders. These disorders include dementia, which is a severe loss of mental capacity, and memory loss. AIDS patients also suffer from a mental disorder that causes them to lose feeling in their arms and legs.

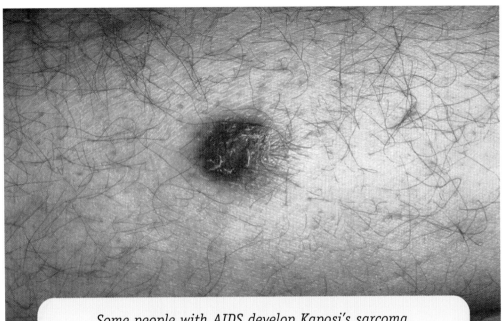

Some people with AIDS develop Kaposi's sarcoma,
a rare skin cancer that causes lesions.

Opportunistic Infections

There are over 100 different germ infections, ranging from mild to severe, that can cause opportunistic infections in an AIDS patient. Examples of opportunistic infections include pneumonia and tuberculosis, or TB. There are twenty-six opportunistic infections that doctors use as a guide in giving a diagnosis of AIDS to a patient.

5

TREATMENT, RESEARCH, AND PREVENTION

Current treatment options for HIV infection and AIDS provide both good and bad news. The bad news is that there are no cures for either disease at the present time. The good news is that modern advances in treatment and research are helping many people with HIV and AIDS to live longer, more productive, and healthier lives.

HIV Treatment

HIV multiplies, or replicates itself, very quickly in an infected person. As HIV multiplies, it weakens the immune system. Medications can help reduce the amount of HIV in your body, as well as slow down the replication of HIV.

The kinds of medications that a doctor prescribes for treatment depend on the individual person and the severity of his or her HIV infection. Doctors design individual treatment plans for each patient. There are several different kinds of medications that you can take for treatment, but it is important to know that no drug treatment can eliminate the spread of HIV from one person to another. A treatment plan is usually determined after the doctor has run a count on your helper T cells, and also on your viral load. Viral load means the amount of HIV that is in your bloodstream. For some people the viral load can be high, meaning a great deal of HIV is present, and for some it can be low.

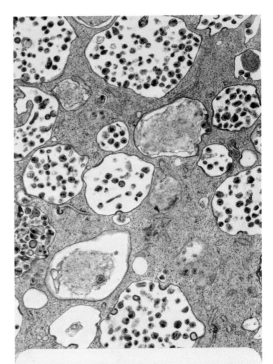

This is a microscopic view of Human Immunodeficiency Virus (HIV).

There are many types of medications for HIV treatment. HIV medications, or anti-HIV drugs, must be approved by the Food and Drug Administration before they can be prescribed. The types of approved anti-HIV drugs are:

- Protease inhibitors—Drugs of this type work to interrupt HIV replication and may keep HIV replication controllable for long periods of time.
- Nucleoside reverse transcriptase inhibitors, or NRTIs—Drugs of this type also interrupt HIV replication, and they may delay the appearance of opportunistic infections in persons with advanced HIV.
- Non-nucleoside reverse transcriptase inhibitors, or NNRTIs—Drugs of this type interrupt HIV replication, but they do not slow down the spread of HIV from cell to cell.

None of these drugs kills HIV, but anti-HIV treatment can reduce the amount of HIV in your body. HIV is a clever virus, and it can change, or mutate, in order to survive. HIV can also become resistant to drug therapy.

Doctors combat this resistance by using a combination of anti-HIV drugs. Using more than one type of drug to treat an illness is called combination therapy. Studies on combination therapy for HIV have shown that it can prevent HIV from mutating, as well as effectively slow down the replication of new HIV organisms.

Doctors tell patients about risks, benefits, and possible side effects of any drug therapy. Side effects are the unexpected and unwanted symptoms that can be caused by taking the drug. Side effects for anti-HIV drugs vary from person to person and drug to drug.

AIDS Treatment

People with AIDS are more open to developing other illnesses. Some of these illnesses can be prevented. Doctors give immunization shots to some AIDS patients. Immunization shots prevent the development of certain kinds of illnesses. Other treatments can cure some of the illnesses. There are several drugs that treat opportunistic infections, or illnesses that are normally mild in a healthy person but that can become dangerous in an AIDS patient.

AIDS patients who develop cancers such as Kaposi's sarcoma are treated with standard cancer treatments. They may also receive shots of specific proteins called alpha interferon. Alpha interferon shots raise the level of proteins in the body, which fights infection.

Research for HIV and AIDS

Research is the single most important area when it comes to conquering diseases. Without research on

HIV and AIDS, the choices for treatment would be very few, and infected people would not be able to live as long. Also, we would not know the important facts about HIV and AIDS which can allow us to avoid becoming infected with it. Researchers are currently looking into further development and testing of HIV vaccines. Dozens of vaccines are being tested on HIV patients throughout the country. Researchers are also investigating new treatment options for AIDS and the infections associated with AIDS.

Prevention

The AIDS epidemic has taken over 16 million lives since it began. Children account for 3.2 million of the 16 million deaths. It is estimated that globally, more than 33 million people are living with HIV or AIDS, and that over 10,000 new infections develop each day. The clearest way of preventing the spread of HIV and AIDS is to avoid the behaviors that can cause HIV. There are steps that you can take now, which will help you to avoid becoming infected with HIV. Always avoid unprotected sexual contact. Do not share hypodermic needles, and use only specially cleaned needles for tattoos or piercings.

Saying No to High-Risk Behavior

At many moments in life, we are faced with decisions that can change us forever. Saying no to sex or drug use can be very difficult, but avoidance of these two behaviors is protection against disease. Your friends, boyfriend or girlfriend, or family members should accept your decisions. You can respond to pressure about sex or drugs by saying things such as:

☺ I am not ready, and since it is my body, I will tell you when I am ready.

☺ I am very sure . . . my answer is no.

☺ I care about you, but I don't want to have sex.

☺ I am taking care of my body, and drugs will harm my body.

☺ I will not break the law, and drugs are illegal.

Saying no can give you more time to figure out exactly who you are and who you want to be, without added pressures. If you should decide to participate in sex, be smart about it. You cannot tell when a partner or friend might have HIV, and in many cases he or she might not know either. Unprotected sex is never safe. The use of latex condoms ensures

The AIDS epidemic has claimed the lives of more than 16 million people, but by working together, we can help stop AIDS from spreading further.

that HIV has fewer chances of being transmitted during sexual activities. Use condoms during any sexual activity, including vaginal, anal, and oral sex.

Looking to the Future

Now that we know what causes AIDS and how to prevent AIDS and HIV infection, we have some control over the outcome of the AIDS epidemic. The choices that each of us makes individually can stop the spread of AIDS.

GLOSSARY

AIDS (acquired immunodeficiency syndrome) Infectious disease caused by HIV. An AIDS diagnosis is given if a person's T cell count is less than 200.

antibody Natural substance made by B cells to fight a particular infection.

asymptomatic The presence of illness without symptoms.

B cell Type of white blood cell that produces antibodies.

dementia A mental disorder.

HIV (human immunodeficiency virus) An infectious virus that causes the eventual development of the disease AIDS.

immune system The body's defense system against illness, disease, and infection.

immunization Using a vaccine to stimulate the immune system to fight infection.

Kaposi's sarcoma (KS) A rare cancer that causes lesions. It is most likely to be found in AIDS patients.

lesion   Scratch, bump, wound, or other abnormality in the tissue of the body.

lymph nodes   Areas where immune reactions occur, and which are found in the neck, armpit, groin, and deep inside the body.

lymphocyte   Term for a type of white blood cell.

lymphoma   A cancer of the lymph nodes.

opportunistic infection   When organisms take advantage of the "opportunity" of a weakened immune system by growing out of control and causing disease.

protease inhibitors   Type of anti-HIV drug.

symptomatic   The presence of illness with symptoms.

T cell   Cell of the immune system.

tuberculosis (TB)   Infection in or outside of the lungs.

viral load   Amount of virus in a tested sample of blood or body fluid.

virus   Germ that needs a living organism in order to become activated to survive and multiply.

white blood cells   Cells of the immune system that protect the body from harmful organisms and substances.

FOR MORE INFORMATION

In the United States

Centers for Disease Control National AIDS Hotline
(800) 342-AIDS (2437)
Spanish: (800) 344-SIDA (7432)
Web site: http://www.cdc.gov/hiv/pubs/facts.htm

Gay Men's Health Crisis
119 West 24th Street
New York, NY 10011
(800) AIDS-NYC (243-7692)
Web site: http://www.gmhc.org

HIV/AIDS Treatment Information Service (ATIS)
P.O. Box 6303
Rockville, MD 20849-6303

(800) HIV-0440 (448-0440)
Web site: http://www.hivatis.org

NAMES Project Foundation (The AIDS Quilt)
310 Townsend Street, Suite 310
San Francisco, CA 94107
(415) 882-5500
Web site: http://www.AIDSQuilt.org

National Minority AIDS Council
1931 13th Street NW
Washington, D.C. 20009
(202) 483-6622
Web site: http://www.nmac.org

In Canada

Canadian AIDS Society
130 Albert Street, Suite 900
Ottawa, ON K1P 5G4
(613) 230-3580
Web site: http://www.cdnaids.ca

Canadian HIV/AIDS Clearinghouse
1565 Carling Avenue, Suite 400
Ottawa, ON K1Z 8R1
(877) 999-7740
Web site: http://www.cpha.ca/clearinghouse_e.htm

FOR FURTHER READING

Brimner, Larry Dane. *The Names Project*. Danbury, CT: Children's Press, 2000.

Forbes, Anna. *Living in a World with AIDS*. New York: Rosen Publishing Group, 1997.

Rust Nash, Carol. *AIDS: Choices for Life*. Springfield, NJ: Enslow Publishers, Inc., 1997.

Shein, Lori. *AIDS*. San Diego, CA: Lucent Books, 1998.

Taylor, Barbara. *Everything You Need to Know About AIDS*. Rev. ed. New York: Rosen Publishing Group, 1998.

INDEX

A

Africa, 26, 37–38
AIDS
    diagnosis of, 11, 40–49
    early cases, 25–26
    history of, 23–36
    and HIV, 7–9, 10–11, 25,
       30, 31
    prevention, 54–56
    spread of, 30–31
    treatment, 53, 54
    worldwide, 37–39
AIDS Memorial Quilt, 33
antibodies, 8, 28, 29, 34, 41,
       42, 43, 44, 45, 47
anti-HIV drugs, 33, 51–53
AZT, 33

B

B cells, 8
blood tests, 11, 28, 36, 40, 41
blood transfusions, 18, 31, 41
body fluids, 13–14, 17, 21
breast-feeding, 14, 16
breast milk, 13, 16–17

C

cancer, 10, 27
Centers for Disease Control
    (CDC), 25, 27, 36
combination drug treatments,
    36, 52
condoms, 15, 31, 55–56

D

drug use, 15, 55
Dugas, Gaetan, 30–31

E

East Asia, 37, 38–39

F

false positive/negative, 45–47
Food and Drug Administration
    (FDA), 33, 44, 51

G

Gallo, Robert, 28–29, 31
gay community, 27, 30
GRID (gay-related immune defi-
    ciency), 27, 30

H

helper T cells, 8, 51
hemophiliacs, 27, 30
HIV, 8–9
  discovery of, 28–29, 30, 31
  history of, 23–36
  how it causes AIDS, 10–21
  how it is spread, 13–17, 18–19
  prevention, 54–56
  replication, 50, 52
  symptoms of, 11–12, 28, 40, 47
  testing for, 29, 34, 40–47
  treatment, 50–53
Hudson, Rock, 31, 35

I

immune system, 7, 8, 9, 10, 11, 12, 47, 48, 50
immunization shots, 53
India, 37, 38
infection, 9, 10, 41, 42, 45, 49, 53
  opportunistic, 10–11, 33, 36, 49, 52, 53
insect bites, 18–19

J

Johnson, Magic, 34

K

Kaposi's sarcoma, 27, 36, 48, 53
kissing, 17, 19

L

lymph nodes, 11–12, 28, 48

M

Mercury, Freddie, 34, 35
Montagnier, Luc, 28–29, 30, 31

N

needles, sharing, 14, 15–16, 40, 54

P

polio vaccines, 24–25
pregnancy, 14, 16, 38
public awareness and education, 32, 34

R

Reagan, Ronald, 32, 34
research, 18, 23, 53–54

S

sex, unprotected, 14–15, 30–31, 40, 54, 55
simian immunodeficiency virus (SIV), 23, 36

T

tattoos and piercings, 14, 16, 41, 54
T cells, 8, 11

V

vaccines, 54
virus, 7–8, 18, 23, 30, 36, 45

W

White House AIDS Summit, 36
White, Ryan, 31, 34, 35

CREDITS

About the Author

Holly Cefrey is a freelance writer and researcher. She has written a number of books on a wide variety of medical topics.

Photo Credits

Cover and chapter backgrounds © NIBSC/Science Photo Library (SPL)/Photo Researchers, Inc.; p. 4 © Jacques M. Chenet/Corbis; p. 14 © Phillip Hayson/Photo Researchers, Inc.; p. 15 © Custom Medical; p. 16 © Mike Malyszko/FPG International; pp. 19, 20, 22 © Pictor; p. 25 © Jack Moebes/Corbis; p. 28 © Reuters/Luciano Mellace/Archive Photos; p. 29 © Photo Researchers, Inc.; p. 32 © Bettmann/Corbis; p. 33 © Lee Sanders/Corbis; p. 35 © Corbis; p. 42 © AP/Worldwide; p. 46 © Richard Nowitz MR/Photo Researchers, Inc.; p. 49 © George Moore, M.D., PhD./Custom Medical; p. 51 © Dr. R. Dourmashkin/SPL/Photo Researchers, Inc.; p. 56 © AP/Worldwide.

Series Design

Evelyn Horovicz

Layout

Geri Giordano